A NOTE FROM PASTOR ROBEY

It takes courage to pick up a booklet like this.

It requires a fervent passion to bring every part of our lives under the rule of Jesus. It takes faith that God's word still speaks in a timeless and life-giving way. I admire the brave step you are taking to invest in your relationship with God in such a critical part of your life. I am also expectant for you. Any part of our lives we bring in line with God's truth will become more vibrant. We are praying for you as you dive into what God says about our finances. How could we not be blessed, by opening more of ourselves up to God? There's no question, it is always an adventure following Jesus. It requires a bold, fervent faith. That's the kind of people we want to be. We are all or nothing!

For His glory,
Pastor Robey

Copyright © 2024 by Robey Barnes

All rights reserved.

First Things: Worshiping God Through Our Giving is a production of City Rev Church. No portion of this book may be reproduced in any form without written permission from the author.

REVEALING JESUS +
REVOLUTIONIZING THE CITY

CITYREV.ORG

TABLE OF CONTENTS

INTRODUCTION 8

CHAPTER 1:
THE ULTIMATE PRETENDER 14

CHAPTER 2:
THE ANCIENT PLAN 22

CHAPTER 3:
THE FOUNDATIONAL PRACTICES 30

CHAPTER 4:
THE IRONCLAD PROMISES 40

CONCLUSION 51

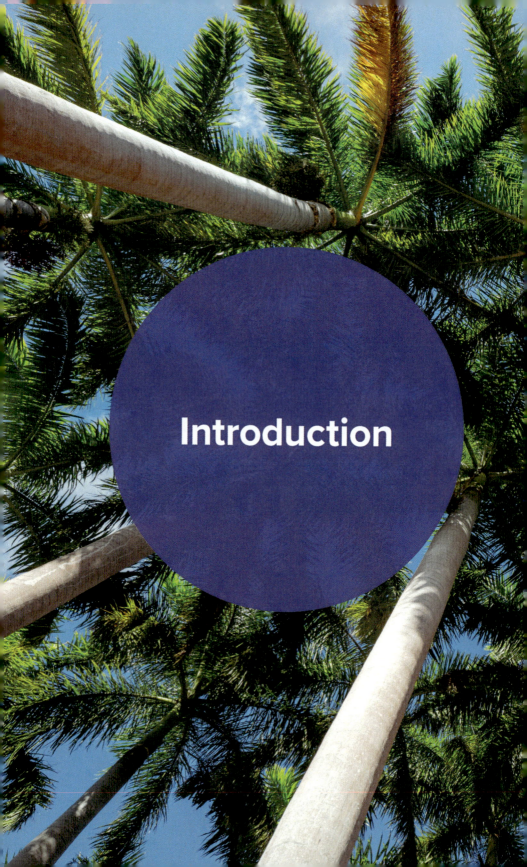

Introduction

Let's start with this: Jesus is the rock. He is the foundation. All other ground is sinking sand (Mt 7:24-27). We believe that. Which means every aspect of our lives must be, first and foremost, calibrated to Jesus. It must be directed by God. It must be under the reign of the true King. Let's put it another way. If I want any part of my life to thrive, then I should align it to God's ways (Is 55:8-9). That is a basic biblical paradigm. If I base any part of my life on anything else, on any other theory or philosophy or strategy, it reveals a divided heart.

It is also only logical to align our lives to God's ways. We believe God created everything. He is the Inventor. All that is in existence comes from His brilliance. Furthermore, He has an agenda for it. He has a purpose and a plan, and He communicates His plan to us in the scripture. He is the source of beauty and truth and life. It is simply the most logical move to align our life to the Designer's designs.

For most facets of our lives, it is not complicated to anchor them to God's ways. We want to center our marriages on Jesus. We want to parent in a way that honors God. We want to see God at work in our careers. But let's be honest, when it comes to God and finances, we have baggage.

If we are going to dig in on the subject of what God says about money, we must first acknowledge a tragic reality. Many of us have hurt and suspicion when it comes to the subject of money in the context of church.

Unfortunately, many people have been in places where money is talked about so coercively that they began to feel that all the church wanted from them was money. Or worse still, many have been in places where the church mishandled money. This is a devastating experience that destroys trust. It leaves many reluctant to even broach the subject at church, and understandably so.

But unfortunately, to not dig into what God teaches us on this subject is deeply problematic. If we shut out what God shows us about money, then we are doomed to wallow in the world's broken perspective on a critical area of our lives.

INTRODUCTION

Maybe that is just what the enemy wants. Our enemy is prowling around, looking for any way to devour us (1 Pt 5:8). He does not want us to have freedom, joy, rest, or abundance. He wants every part of our existence to be enslaved, shriveled and racked with fear. So what better way to leave our lives in joyless financial brokenness, then to intimidate us into avoiding what the Bible says on the subject. That way our enemy keeps us locked in idolatry and entangled in the oppression of things like greed, envy, vanity and self-reliance. We miss the freedom and life Christ came to bring us.

We stand against all of those weapons and schemes! We defy the enemy's plans to leave our lives in shambles. We want to be trees planted by living water, guzzling down the pure, nourishing, life-giving truths from God's word. We want to experience the Creator's truth enlivening every branch of our lives. God wants us to thrive. Why would we not let God have access to every part of us, especially one as pivotal as our finances?

I remember we were doing a sermon series teaching on Bible passages where Jesus talked about money. There are many to choose from but we picked 4 different teachings. By the third week, someone put a note in the giving box. It said, "Can we stop talking about money and get back to talking about Jesus and the Bible?" Unfortunately, the note was anonymous. If there had been a way to contact them I would have explained the dilemma that created for me. They were saying they didn't want to talk about money and only wanted to focus on Jesus and the Bible. But what about the parts of the Bible where Jesus is talking about money?

Sidestepping passages of the Bible about money redacts whole sections of the Bible. If we are going to be people that stand firm on the word of God, we must study what the Bible says about everything.

If we are going to be people who follow Jesus, we need to be ready to follow what Jesus says about money. Jesus says that He came to give us life abundantly (Jn 10:10). So to avoid what Jesus taught on money is to miss out on the abundance He is leading us into.

Let me be direct. One reason it's hard to talk about money in church is because it seems self-serving for the church to do that. What then is the alternative? If we do not talk about it, there are deep consequences in our lives. If we never study what the Bible says about money, we never learn how the Creator designed money to be handled. We are missing out on the promises from God; worse still, we are likely leaving destructive forces like self-reliance, materialism and greed unaddressed in our lives.

Let's take it a step further. If we never address what God says about money, then a notorious and deadly idol will be left standing. Idolatry always destroys. We are a people that have no other God, but the Lord. He is jealous for us, and like a husband for His bride, He rightfully will not stand for us having divided affections. We do not dare leave finances untouched in our discussions.

To build the financial side of my life on God's ways means I will be breaking with the conventions of our world. I will be doing things that most everyone around me does not do. Like everything with God, I will be operating in faith. It is about trusting that He is in control not me. It is trusting that He provides, not me. When it comes to faith and our finances, that is really scary.

This is the biblical reality we must wrestle with. We are told that without faith it is impossible to please Him (Heb 11:6). Do we have faith? Many years ago I witnessed someone with true faith in God as a provider, and it deeply impacted me.

When I was about seven years old, my Great Aunt Jane came and stayed at our house. It was my mom's aunt, and I had never met her before. My parents explained to me that she and my great uncle were missionaries in Korea and she needed serious eye surgery. She was coming to South Florida for the specialists at the famous Bascom Palmer Eye Institute.

INTRODUCTION

Great Aunt Jane is a faith missionary. That means she and my great uncle did not seek out committed financial support. They prayerfully seek the Lord, and wait for His provision. They follow Him day by day, trusting that He will work out the details of their provision. They usually have no indication where the provision is going to come from. Think about that. They lived with no financial safety net, other than the provision of God. But by this point in their lives, they had seen Jesus provide so many times that this was second nature for them. There was no questioning that God would come through.

So when Aunt Jane showed up to our house, my parents quickly realized that she had not brought any money with her for the procedure! How was she going to pay for this eye surgery? They gently asked her what she planned. She calmly responded that she knew Jesus would provide. That was her entire plan. I don't believe this is always God's strategy for us. This was how they were called to live. It demonstrated the powerful reality of God's provision.

So how did this play out? Sure enough, money started showing up at our house. Though she never asked, people somehow found out that she was there and had felt led by God to send money to help. We marveled at how God was responding to her humble reliance on Him.

The day for the surgery came, and it was a significant enough procedure that it required her to stay in the hospital for a few days. When she was being discharged, she and my mother met with the financial representative. Aunt Jane had brought an envelope with all the money people had mailed her and hoped it would be enough. What do you think happened? You are probably thinking the surgery was the exact amount God sent her. That's not what happened.

The financial representative told her and my mother that the entire cost for the surgery had been paid for in full! They do not know who, but someone had covered the cost of the entire surgery. But wait, what about all the money she had been receiving in the mail for the surgery? Incredibly, she would be ending this trip financially net-positive. She not only got the surgery she desperately needed, but would be going home with more than she came with.

Eventually, we dropped Aunt Jane off at the airport. When we went in to straighten up her room, we found an envelope on the dresser. It was all the money she had received since she had arrived. With it was a note. She was leaving this money to go towards any needs our family may have or for the needs of the ministry my parents worked for. Incredible.

Why would she do that? Surely there were many other needs she had back in Korea. But when you've seen Jesus come through for you over and over, what do you need money for? He's always there ready to supply her needs in abundance. If she has Jesus, what does she need that envelope of money for?

I still marvel at that story. It seems like something that only happens to super-Christians. But there's no such thing as that. There are just disciples. We are all unlikely people transformed by the work of Jesus and filled with the Holy Spirit.

> God invites us to have faith. He is more than capable of responding in ways that are beyond our imagination.

CHAPTER 1

The Ultimate Pretender

Jesus' famous Sermon on the Mount contains words that have literally changed planet earth. It contains the golden rule and the Lord's Prayer. The phrase "the straight and narrow," comes from a parable in the sermon. It is where we find His famous parable about those who built their houses on the sand and the rock. We are taught about being salt and light and loving our enemies. And this is just scratching the surface. The world hasn't been the same since He spoke those words.

Right in the middle of the sermon, Jesus gave us one of the most profound teachings on money. It's straight forward. It's direct. And it bores down into the core of the issue:

> "No one can serve two masters, for either he will hate the one and love the other, or he will be devoted to the one and despise the other. You cannot serve God and money." (Mt 6:24)

Essentially, He is saying at some point every Christian must have a showdown with money. We can't serve both. So which is it? Who do we worship: the Living God or money?

Why does Jesus force this distinction? We all have a relationship with money. But we often separate money into a different category than the spiritual part of our lives. We often think of money as earthly and pragmatic. However, that is not what Jesus taught.

> Money is far more spiritual than we think. According to Jesus, money is a worship issue.

CHAPTER 1

MONEY AS AN IDOL

Money makes promises. Think of all the things it says it will do. Money supposedly provides for our needs. We think we can't live without money. It is how we get the necessities. Money also promises to supply pleasure and fun. The prospect of getting a lump sum of money is enticing. It tantalizes us with all the thrilling things we could buy. Money says it will increase our status and significance. We naturally feel more impressive and accomplished if we have more money and the stuff that comes with it. Money looks like it increases stability and security. We naturally think, "as long as I have enough money, I will be ok." Now stop and consider that list: provision, joy, significance, security. Those are things that only God can do. Anything else that makes those claims is a false god.

> Money is the most common idol in our culture and maybe in history.

It is commonplace to assume more money means more of all the best parts of life. And so much of our culture is actually built on that premise. We say things like, "money makes the world go round." It is telling that such a common phrase is essentially stating that the universe revolves around money. We don't mean it literally, but it reveals our cultural idol. We consciously know it's not true but there are deep down presuppositions that betray those thoughts.

In reality money is like every other idol. It will fail us. It is not infallible and all powerful. That new thing we bought breaks or goes out of style. The economy shifts and we are suddenly in a vulnerable situation. We finally have saved up enough to make that big purchase and an unexpected bill comes along. Money seems big and strong, but it is actually quite fragile. And no amount of it can make us feel totally safe. No amount of it can ensure joy. It never quite satisfies. It keeps us on the hamster wheel of still wanting more. Idols cannot do what God can do. And the tricking thing is idols are usually not bad things. They are usually good things that we put God-like expectations on.

It is not just that idols always fail. Idols are severely destructive. They are devastating to those that have them. If we leave the idol of money active in our hearts it shreds us. Money demands that we serve it. It crushes us under the weight of anxiety that we do not have enough. It never relieves those fears, it only stokes it into an unbearable furnace. It seduces us into finding momentary happiness by buying more things. This is until we are so bloated by the glitter of temporary things, we are left over-indulged and bored. Or we are crushed by the financial debts it has put us under. Spending for happiness is like a drug dealer that gets us hooked and craving another hit.

Money as an idol is vile and cruel. It demands we chase it all the while we are distracted from the most beautiful gifts in our lives. One example of this could be someone feverishly chasing a career and an increased salary, all the while missing the treasures of priceless moments with their family? I'm not talking about the extravagant vacation money bought. I mean the otherwise unremarkable Thursday night, where a family laughed together until tears ran down their cheeks. The idol of money will keep us too busy, too distracted and too stressed for moments like that. With money as an idol, it dangles more in front of us, all the while it is robbing us.

Yet, the most sinister aspect of money as an idol is that it all feels so normal. We may be operating like everyone else we know. We can go through life numb to the reality that we are relying on the

CHAPTER 1

wrong things. We can completely miss the consequences of putting our hopes in a pretend god. We get so used to our idols, that we don't realize they are there.

TEARING DOWN THE IDOL

Uprooting and destroying idols in our lives is an essential part of thriving. Over and over in the Bible, God warns us how ignoring idols in our lives is a recipe for emptiness, dryness and brokenness. Jeremiah describes the sin of idolatry like this, "for my people have committed two evils: they have forsaken me, the fountain of living waters, and hewed out cisterns for themselves, broken cisterns that can hold no water." (2:13). Not only do idols come up empty when we need them, idols also keep us from drinking deeply from the source of life. If we rely on something as shaky as money for things as important as significance, security and joy, we will have lives tainted with envy, anxiety and disappointment.

If money is an idol, then money is a worship issue. It is deeply ingrained into the spiritual part of our lives. If money is kept in its rightful place, it is not a bad thing. God has much to say about money. He tells us what some of the most lifegiving uses of money are. He teaches us how to manage it wisely. He reveals secrets about how to maximize joy and eliminate anxiety. He tells us how to avoid letting our possessions possess us. But all of this is built on one thing: we must first dethrone money.

God gives us a foundational practice to overthrow money. It forces us to make a decision between God and money. It is a critical step that is concrete. It makes it nearly impossible to fake. It forces us to put aside all rationalizing and have a definitive action for choosing what God we serve. And it forces us to take a step of faith in the Almighty.

That foundational practice is giving financially back to God first before anything else. We will dig into that in the next chapter. But before we do, I want to share a testimony from someone in our church.

One Sunday, after the services, a man named Juan approached me. He said, "today you were talking about what the Bible says about giving. I have to tell you what happened to me earlier this week." He told me that he was sitting with his cousin, who is also a Christian. The subject of finances came up. In their discussion, the cousin asked Juan if he financially gave back to the Lord. Juan told him that he gave on occasion but it wasn't a regular part of his life. The cousin lovingly challenged him on the subject.

> He reminded Juan of what Jesus said, "where your treasure is, there your heart will be also."

The heart follows the treasure. He challenged Juan to give a full 10% of his income back to God in faith. Juan was impacted by it. And the idea didn't leave him for the next several days. Finally, he felt compelled to take a step. He went online and for the first time gave a full tithe back to God.

CHAPTER 1

Juan looked at me dead in the eye and said, "I will never forget what I felt at that moment. It was like a hand was reaching down into my heart and lifted a huge weight off of me. I have never felt anything like it." For the first time Juan had totally surrendered his finances to the Lord. God was taking the burden of providing for him. An idol fell that day.

This chapter focused on exposing money as one of the most notorious false gods. Like all idols it promises to give us life, but when we depend on it to do what only God can do, it always fails us. It is so deadly as an idol, that we cannot possibly leave it standing in our lives.

> We must be proactive in dethroning the pretend god. And the true Living God gives us a clear tangible way to do that. Let's see what God's plan is for removing the reliance on money in our lives.

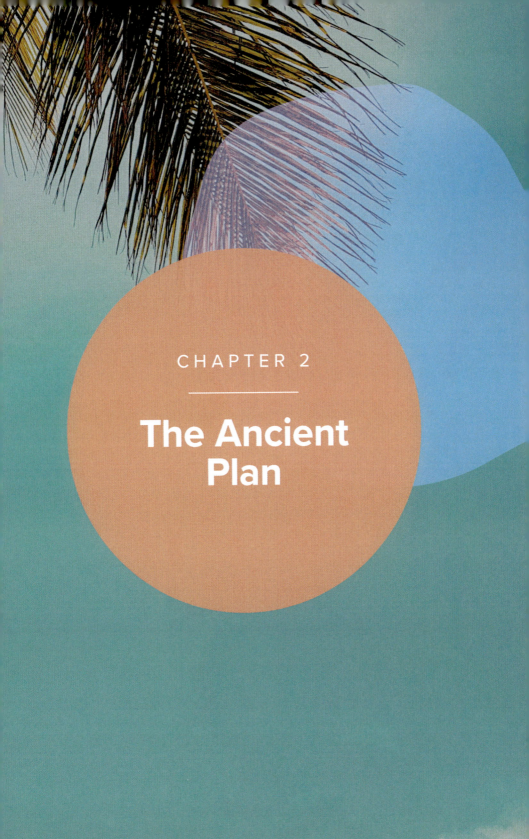

CHAPTER 2

The Ancient Plan

God's ancient plan for our finances starts in a place that is absolutely counter-intuitive to our culture. It starts with giving back to Him. This is a dramatic statement of where our chief value and treasure is. It is a pivotal faith step that catapults the rest of our being in the direction of the Father. It violently disrupts the infantile view that what we need in life is more money. And it is an act of rebellion and defiance against the enemy's attempt to poison our souls with the preoccupation of money. The love of money is the root of all kinds of evils. (1 Tm 6:10)

How do we ensure money is not poisoning us? What is God's plan for us to overthrow the money's control over our lives? To do this we can dig into one of the prophets.

A TIME FOR REVIVAL

The short book of Malachi is the final word in the Old Testament. It's a powerful crescendo. It is the story of a generation that experienced a revival. The prophet Malachi has strong words for God's people. He calls them to repentance. It beautifully records their return to the Lord by saying, "a book of remembrance was written before Him of those who feared the Lord and esteemed His name." (Mal 3:16). What a powerful way to end the dramatic saga of the Old Testament.

The book opens up with a strong rebuke of the spiritual leaders. He chastises them for allowing weak, half-hearted worship among the people. God's people were just going through the motions. He was not getting the best from them. They were giving Him their leftovers. There was no fear of the Lord. Their worship was insincere and apathetic.

Interestingly, God says it's the priest's fault. He says that the priests tolerating such worship is equivalent to "despising His name." He says if the priests do not listen to Him and change course that He will, "send the curse upon you and I will curse your blessings... I will rebuke your offspring, and spread dung on your faces, the dung of

CHAPTER 2

your offerings, and you shall be taken away with it." (2:2-3) Whoa! God is certainly restoring a fear of the Lord to His people. And he's starting with those who are supposed to be the spiritual leaders.

How is this practically playing out with the priests? What is the fake worship they are allowing? Here is what God says:

> "You say, 'How have we despised your name?' By offering polluted food upon my altar. But you say, 'How have we polluted you?' By saying that the Lord's table may be despised. When you offer blind animals in sacrifice, is that not evil? And when you offer those that are lame or sick, is that not evil? Present that to your governor; will he accept you or show you favor? says the Lord of hosts." (Mal 1:6-8)

The people are bringing offerings that are less than their best. They are not bringing the best of their flocks. It is not unblemished lambs. They are offering livestock that are blind or lame or sick. He says that a gift like that would be an insult to your governor and yet they think that will not offend the Almighty? He calls them to repent of such weak and apathetic worship. In fact, He puts it like this, "Cursed be the cheat who has a male in His flock, and vows it, and yet sacrifices to the Lord what is blemished. For I am a great King, says the Lord of hosts, and my name will be feared among the nations." (Mal 1:14) And specifically He holds the priests responsible for allowing this.

At the end of the rebuke of the spiritual leaders and the people, He calls them to return to Him. They ask God what they should do to return. What is the action step to demonstrate their fear of the Lord? This is what God says. Please don't skim past this. These are powerful words straight from God:

"For I the Lord do not change; therefore you, O children of Jacob, are not consumed. From the days of your fathers you have turned aside from my statutes and have not kept them. Return to me, and I will return to you, says the Lord of hosts. But you say, 'How shall we return?' Will man rob God? Yet you are robbing me. But you say, 'How have we robbed you?' In your tithes and contributions. You are cursed with a curse, for you are robbing me, the whole nation of you. Bring the full tithe into the storehouse, that there may be food in my house. And thereby put me to the test, says the Lord of hosts, if I will not open the windows of heaven for you and pour down for you a blessing until there is no more need." (Mal 3:6-10)

How should they return to the Lord? What is God prescribing for a people turning their hearts to God? Maybe it should be a robust worship service with passionate singing. Maybe they pray and praise with tears and sing late into the night. Or maybe it should be a week-long series of bible study and worship music every night. No. It's none of those things. There is nothing wrong with them. But that doesn't get right to the heart. That does not pry their fingers off the idols they were clutching. That is not God's plan for them to crush the false gods that have stolen their affections. God knows what legitimate repentance looks like.

> He says bring the full tithe into the storehouse.

CHAPTER 2

Notice that God said that to fail to bring a tithe was robbing Him. He was not saying, "have a more generous posture towards me." It is not a matter of giving a little extra to God. This was not worded as an act of generosity. He was saying you are being unfaithful to neglect bringing the tithe to the temple. It belongs to God. He doesn't call them stingy. He's not saying they are being miserly and need to share more. He says they are robbers.

This passage in Malachi 3 is not a teaching on generosity. Generosity is an important part of our lives. It is something God wants to stir up in us as an outflow of the gospel. Generosity is about our recalibration to the world He sent us to. It's an act of self-sacrifice and love for others. But, the practice of first giving back to the Lord is not about generosity. It is about faithfulness. If generosity is about recalibrating ourselves to our world, giving back to God is about a recalibration to Him.

GIVING AS WORSHIP

We often don't think about offering money to God as something associated with worship. When we think about worship, we typically think about singing. And that is certainly an important practice we are commanded to do. It is an important part of our corporate and private worship to God. But, let's not miss out on the essence of worship. It is always fundamentally about offering something back to God. So when we sing it is not for us. It is one of the many ways we make an offering to Him. We are giving Him praise.

Worship is not about what we get out of it, worship is about what we give. If our spirituality is about what we get out of it, then we misunderstand worship. We think it is something for us. If that is our framework for worship, is it even worship at all? Something is off if singing to God is about how it makes me feel, or if biblical teaching is tips for me to live the life that I want. If worship is for me, then it is not an act of submission and surrender to a Sovereign God.

So it is unfortunate, and even deeply concerning that giving financially back to God is so disconnected from our understanding of worship. One of the first expressions of worship mentioned in the Bible is Cain and Abel bringing an offering to God (Gn 4). Throughout the Bible giving financially back to God is a fundamental part of our worship.

That is why it is so pivotal to draw a sharp distinction about faithfully giving back to God and generosity. Giving back to God is not an extra. It's not something we are doing above and beyond out of the kindness of our hearts.

> Giving to God is a faithful declaration of who is first in our lives. We are not first in our lives. The government is not first in our lives. Our financial dreams are not first in our lives. Our vacations and clothes and electronics are not first in our lives. Even food and shelter are not first in our lives.
>
> **GOD ALONE IS GOD. HE IS FIRST.**

CHAPTER 2

Let's acknowledge giving back to the Lord is a challenging step. This practice is simultaneously both difficult and essential because money is an idol. Here's one example of what God says, "The best of the firstfruits of your ground you shall bring into the house of the Lord your God" (Ex 23:19). God is first, He is our provider, protector and source of life. Before anything else, we give back to Him.

Giving financially back to God cannot be skipped. It is not optional. It is a matter of faithfulness. It is a matter of tearing down idols. It cannot be skipped and it cannot be delayed. It is tempting to think, "I will be generous back to God one day when I've made good money." But this is not about charitable generosity. This is a worship issue. It is about dethroning an idol. Here is how God addresses that, "Beware lest you say in your heart, 'My power and the might of my hand have gotten me this wealth.' You shall remember the Lord your God, for it is He who gives you power to get wealth" (Dt :17-18).

Some think that giving financially is just one of the ways a Christian can serve God. I've heard it said like this: some people are generous with their time, some are generous with their talents, and then there are some who are generous with their treasures. There is no doubt that there are all kinds of ways to be generous. Generosity is not just about money. We want generosity to infiltrate every part of our lives. But there is something in particular God wants us to do with our finances, because it is a particularly notorious idol. Giving back to God is not optional. It is critical. It is a fight for the worship of our hearts.

In this chapter we discussed God's timeless principle of giving back to Him. It is this pivotal practice that God commanded us to do from the very beginning. It is a fundamental act of worship that God profoundly uses in our lives. In the next chapter we will look at how God teaches us to practice this.

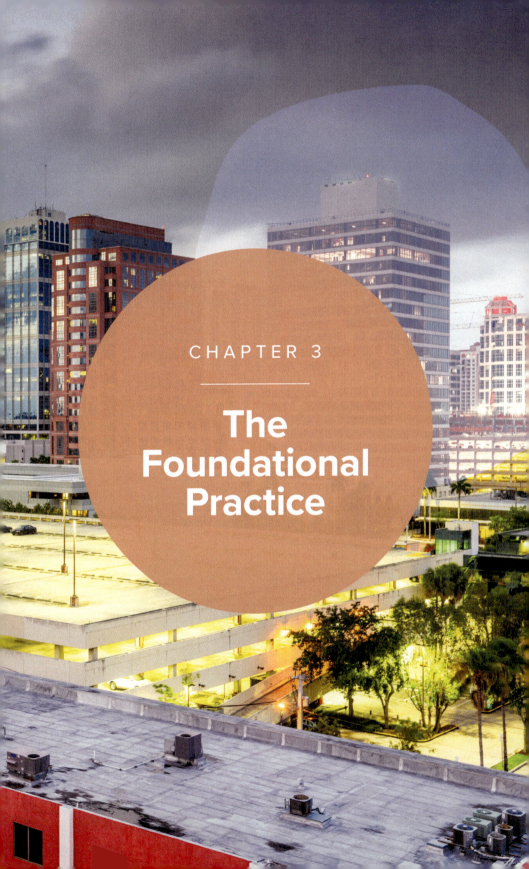

CHAPTER 3

The Foundational Practice

THE FOUNDATIONAL PRACTICE

A tithe is a mathematical term for a tenth. Thinking in these increments is not completely foreign to us. It is a common rule of thumb to set aside 10% of one's income for saving for the future. It should not be strange then to think in a similar way about giving back to God. If we save for the future, would we not give back a significant percentage of our income to the One who holds our future in His hands? We do not tithe because of the logic behind it. We tithe because God commands us to do it.

The idea of the tithe stretches back long before the time of Moses and the law. It appears in a fascinating passage about Abraham. It was the precise amount Abraham gave to the mysterious High Priest Melchizedek (Gn 14:18-20). This was when Israel was merely a promise. The father of God's people is giving a tithe to the high priest and prince of a city called Salem. It is not only the earliest mention of the city Jerusalem. But Salem literally means, "peace." So Abraham is tithing to the prince of peace! This figure seems to appear without warning and out of nowhere. Many believe it is a pre-incarnate appearance of Jesus! This is a majorly significant passage. All of this to say, the tithe predates the law. It is a framework God's people used from early on.

The tithe was then affirmed explicitly in the law of Moses. These verses are a few examples of this command:

Leviticus 27:30, "Every tithe of the land, whether of the seed of the land or of the fruit of the trees, is the Lord's; it is holy to the Lord."

Deuteronomy 14:22, "You shall tithe all the yield of your seed that comes from the field year by year."

CHAPTER 3

The first 10% of what they earned was taken to the storehouse and given back to God.

What is this storehouse? The storehouse was a literal place in the temple where they stored the resources that were given. The leaders in the temple, the priests and levites, were then responsible to distribute these resources to the appropriate needs in the community. "Then all Judah brought the tithe of the grain, wine, and oil into the storehouses. And I appointed as treasurers over the storehouses." (Neh 13:12-13) The law commanded them to set aside the first 10% and bring it to the storehouse.

THE TITHE AND THE NEW TESTAMENT

But everything is different after Jesus. We are part of a glorious new covenant of grace. So is giving a literal 10% the binding amount Christians have to use today? This is an important question. To fall back under the law is to neglect to walk in the power of the Gospel. There is so much of the law we no longer follow. We no longer eat kosher or make sacrifices. So what do we do with this part of the Old Testament?

God is clear, Jesus has completely fulfilled the law on our behalf. Our law is now Christ (1 Cor 9:21, Gal 6:2). We are no longer bound to it. We are bound to Jesus. Because of the complete forgiveness through Jesus, the Holy Spirit is doing something exceedingly more profound in us. He is not simply helping us live up to a moral code. God is transforming us. We are not just a better version of ourselves. We are new creations (2 Cor 5:17)! He is doing something in us that the law could never accomplish. He is re-creating us to be like Him. He is making us like Jesus (Rom 8:29).

Then what do we do with the law? Paul tells us the Old Testament law is beneficial for us because it is like a teacher, helping us learn the heart of God (Gal 3:24-26). It guarded us so that sin didn't destroy us. But now, think of what is possible because of the work of Christ. We have the Spirit of the Almighty God living in us! The Creator God is at work on us from the inside out. His power takes us far beyond what the Law ever could. The Gospel does not make us less righteous. Christ did not free us so that we could walk in the flesh! (Gal 5:13) His grace is not given so that sin increases (Rom 6:1-4). Sin has been put to death!

I would never say, "now that I am under grace I follow the Ten Commandments less. Before when I was under the law I never murdered anyone. But now in Christ I have the freedom to murder a little." Of course not! Now that I am under grace, I take it even further. Not only do I never murder, I root out hatred and bitterness, which Jesus tells me is murder in the heart (Mt 6:21-22). The difference with the new covenant is not that I no longer live righteously. It is that I desire righteousness (Mt 5:6). It is written on my heart (Jer 31:33).

Let's look at another example. Under the law of Moses, there were certain foods God's people couldn't eat, like pork (Lv 11). After Jesus became the Savior and perfectly fulfilled the law for us, Peter is specifically instructed that all foods are now clean (Acts 10). What is the purpose of this? Is it for our enjoyment? No, there is something far more significant happening. We are not free from the law for the sake of the flesh. Through the law God said, "be holy as I am holy." (Lv 11:44) Through Jesus, God is giving us more than commands to do that. He is recreating us into Christ's image (Rom 8:29). Our new frame of reference is Jesus not the law. So when it comes to food, we operate out of love. So we willingly restrict our freedom on what we eat for the sake of others (Rom 14:13-23). While we are not made holy by what we eat or don't eat, even when we eat we use it as an opportunity to worship God. (1 Tm 4:1-5) No matter what we eat or drink, we do it for the glory of God (1 Cor 10:31).

CHAPTER 3

So what does it look like to be financially faithful in light of the Gospel?

We can at least start with this, it will certainly not be less than the law. The Gospel takes us farther. Some will point out that the word "tithe" is hardly used in the New Testament. And they are correct. It is usually mentioned in reference to the Pharisees (e.g. Mt 23:23). So then what do we see in reference to New Testament giving? Here are some examples:

"Jesus looked up and saw the rich putting their gifts into the offering box, and He saw a poor widow put in two small copper coins. And He said, "Truly, I tell you, this poor widow has put in more than all of them. For they all contributed out of their abundance, but she out of her poverty put in all she had to live on." (Lk 21:1-4)

"And Zacchaeus stood and said to the Lord, "Behold, Lord, the half of my goods I give to the poor. And if I have defrauded anyone of anything, I restore it fourfold." And Jesus said to him, "Today salvation has come to this house, since he also is a son of Abraham." (Lk 19:8-9)

"And Jesus, looking at him, loved him, and said to him, "You lack one thing: go, sell all that you have and give to the poor, and you will have treasure in heaven; and come, follow me." (Mk 10:21)

Their reaction to Jesus is dramatic! These individuals understand what it means to follow Jesus. It is all or nothing. It is in line with what Jesus says about following Him. And if we're going to follow Jesus, we need to count the cost. He says, "So therefore, any one of you who does not renounce all that he has cannot be my disciple." (Lk 14:33)

Why does Jesus use such strong language? It is because we are becoming like Jesus. So we primarily ask how much Jesus gave. We know that answer. Jesus expended Himself entirely for us. So to be His disciple, we give all we have back to Him. We are completely His. We are no longer our own. We have been bought with a price (1 Cor 6:19-20).

This is why even after the catch of a lifetime, Peter, Andrew, James and John left their nets behind to follow Jesus (Lk 5:1-11). It is why when Jesus called Matthew, he got up immediately and left the tax booth and everything behind (Lk 5:27-28). It is the reason the early church sold their possessions and brought it to the church leaders to distribute (Acts 4:34-35).

It is true we do not see a tithe in the New Testament. It is always more. We never see less than a tithe. The power of Jesus in our lives takes us so far beyond what the law could do.

Christian, to be a disciple is to have surrendered everything we have to Jesus. If we were under the law, a tithe would be the limit. But for us who are in Christ, tithing is a minimum. Giving 10% of our income to the storehouse is the starting block. It's the training wheels until our hearts catch up.

This is how the ancient church, our spiritual mothers and fathers, taught giving. The second century church father, Irenaeus said,

"And for this reason they (the Jews) had indeed the tithes of their goods consecrated to Him, but those who received liberty [by the work of Jesus] set aside all their possessions for the Lord's purposes, bestowing joyfully and freely not the less valuable portions of their property, since they have the hope of better things [hereafter]; as the poor widow acted who cast all her living into the treasury of God." (Irenaeus, ca. AD 180)

Irenaeus says that the model is not the law, it is the widow who put two pennies into the temple treasury. When Jesus saw it, He stopped the disciples and essentially said, "that's it. She gets it." Jesus gave all He had for us. So it is not surprising He wanted to highlight this woman who gave all she had back to God

THE MODERN CHALLENGE WITH THE TITHE

There are a few challenges with the biblical teaching of the tithe. The first is it is hard to hear from the church. It feels self-serving. We are tempted to say, "Of course you want people to give 10% of their income to the church. That's how the church stays running." In transparency, that obvious reality makes it tempting to back away from teaching the Bible. But remember what God said to the priests in Malachi 1 and 2?

THE FOUNDATIONAL PRACTICE

"And now, O priests, this command is for you. If you will not listen, if you will not take it to heart to give honor to my name, says the Lord of hosts, then I will send the curse upon you and I will curse your blessings. Indeed, I have already cursed them, because you do not lay it to heart." (Mal 2:1-2)

So for pastors or church leaders, what are our options? We must pick between the fear of God or the fear of man. We must fear the Lord!

Christian, hear the word of God, "Bring the full tithe into the storehouse (3:10)." If not, we are robbing God. It is not a matter of generosity. It is not part of your charitable giving. We give the tithe to our church, but it is not chiefly about our church. It is not just because we believe in the work that our church is doing. It is not because the church is one of the non-profits we believe in. This is about God. This is worship. It is a matter of faithfulness. When we bring the first 10% to God, we express that God has preeminence in our lives. We exercise our dependence on Him. And in the process, we are bringing down an idol.

This brings us to the second challenge. And this one is the bigger one: how do we possibly transition to giving 10% of our income back to God? Most people feel like they do not have enough money right now to begin with. Where are we going to find an extra 10%? And that is exactly the point. This is not extra. It is first. This is where we contemplate the rest of that Malachi 3 passage:

"Bring the full tithe into the storehouse, that there may be food in my house. And thereby put me to the test, says the Lord of hosts, if I will not open the windows of heaven for you and pour down for you a blessing until there is no more need." (Mal 3:10)

CHAPTER 3

This is a critical and powerful step of faith. It all comes back to the promises of God. That's the incredible news. God has stunning, life-giving promises attached to this ancient practice.

To tithe means we are not giving leftovers. In fact, if we are giving our "firstfruits." We will start our budget with the tithe. Before money is taken out for the government or set aside for the future or anything else. As we work through the rest of our budget, it forces us to confront the things we think we need. We will be forced to downgrade what we once considered necessities and call them what they are: luxuries. It forces us to learn to gain self-control over our flesh and say "no" to things it demands us to spend on. It requires faith. This may seem extreme, but Jesus told us that is the only way to follow Him! There's no holding back. This is what we signed up for when we made Jesus our King and our Savior.

In this chapter, we explored the faithfulness of God's people from the beginning of Genesis all the way into the early generations of church history. But what kind of generation will we be? May we be a generation that holds the line!

Let us not be remembered as those that chose to worship our God only so far as it makes us feel comfortable.

Is our faith so small that we cannot trust God with money? Is that the extent of our faith? If so, then perhaps God is nothing more than a spiritual vitamin that boosts what we think is an otherwise healthy life. No! He is life itself. We are nothing without Him! He is everything. He is all. There is none beside Him. We believe what we sing. It is not just lip service. So we hold nothing back!

Lastly, don't forget, there are promises attached to this aggressive step of faith. We are obedient and He "pours" out blessing. Let's see what the God of the universe promises us.

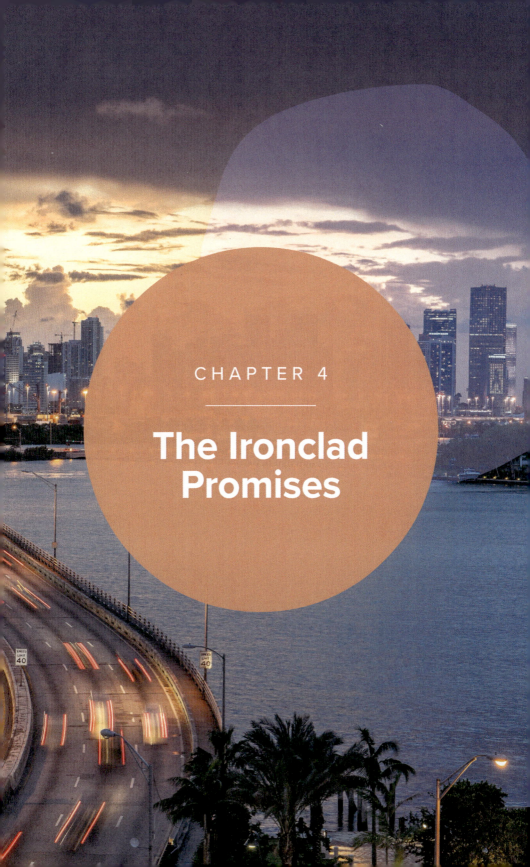

CHAPTER 4

The Ironclad Promises

We have discussed the biblical framework for giving back to the Lord. God's plan for finances starts with giving back to God. That is not an issue of generosity. It is a matter of faithful worship. And if we are following the biblical pattern, 10% is not a suggestion or a maximum. For us who are being transformed into the image of the Son, it is a starting place.

Understandably, for many this seems impossible. Making a jump in one's personal finances to give 10% back to the Lord, seems irresponsibly risky and irreparably disruptive to our plans and goals. But Christian, what in God's word ever told you that following Jesus would mean a comfortable life? Did Jesus ever suggest we would be free from situations that demanded courageous faith? That is not your path, Christian! We are prepared that we will face down kings, giants, the dens of lions and fiery furnaces.

> **The call to a daring life is bolstered by God's promises. He may call us to a fiery furnace, but He will walk in the flames with us.**

As we join those who have gone before us in momentous steps of faith, we will see the power of the same God on our behalf. We will see waters part and walls fall down. Let's not live lives that only see the product of our own efforts. We intend to live in a way that proves to the world the power of our God.

So if He has called us to steps of faith concerning our finances, then we can know there are life-changing miracles He has promised to do. Let's be reminded of His promises and live like it is true.

CHAPTER 4

GOD PROMISES TO PROVIDE

Remember what God said happens when we faithfully give back to Him. Malachi 3:10 says:

> "Bring the full tithe into the storehouse, that there may be food in my house. And thereby put me to the test, says the Lord of hosts, if I will not open the windows of heaven for you and pour down for you a blessing until there is no more need."

God actually says to test Him. This is a rare thing to hear from God. He is basically saying, "Let's have a go. You give and see if I don't pour down blessings on you." Let's agree that there is not a single competition you are going to win against God. This is definitely one you want Him to win!

This is similar to what God says in Haggai 1. The people of God have neglected to prioritize God financially. They have gotten distracted, "busying themselves with their own houses." (1:9) And what are the consequences of this? He says,

> "Now, therefore, thus says the Lord of hosts: Consider your ways. You have sown much, and harvested little. You eat, but you never have enough; you drink, but you never have your fill. You clothe yourselves, but no one is warm. And he who earns wages does so to put them into a bag with holes."

But when they turn back to the Lord, and prioritize Him again, He says,

"Is the seed yet in the barn? Indeed, the vine, the fig tree, the pomegranate, and the olive tree have yielded nothing. But from this day on I will bless you."

He will provide. But often He must first teach us to rely on Him for provision. He loves us too much to let us live in under the suffocating and crushing delusion of self-dependency. We have God! Why do we depend on ourselves?

Remember what Jesus says in Matthew 6.

> He says, "why are you so worried about how you are going to provide for yourself? Look at the birds! The Father provides for the birds and you are so much more valuable than they are."

How valuable are you to God? His love is so immense for you, it takes a miracle for you to comprehend the depths and height and lengths and breadth (Eph 3:17-19). Do you see what kind of love the Father has? He calls you a son or daughter (1 Jn 3:1). And that is who you are.

You've been adopted into His family. He can't help Himself towards you. You're His child because of the work of Jesus. So He will work all things together for good. He loves you so much, He didn't spare His own Son. Would He hold anything else back from you? (Rom 8:12-39) God will provide. It's a guarantee.

GOD PROMISES TO OUT-GIVE YOU

This point needs to be made as clear as possible. When we take a step of faith and give financially to God, the promise in scripture is that He gives back to us even more than we gave. This is not a gimmick and it is not a trick. It's a wonderful, miraculous, significant aspect of the faith walk with God. It's a powerful and intimate part of the journey that He wants to experience with you. It's not just in Malachi 3. Look what Jesus says in Luke, "Give, and it will be given to you. Good measure, pressed down, shaken together, running over, will be put into your lap. For with the measure you use it will be measured back to you." (Lk 6:38)

How does this work? Does this mean that if I give more to God, I will get rich? The promise is actually much deeper and more profound than that. You know this, but it is easy to forget: getting richer does not mean getting happier. Many who have won the lottery have said it ruined their lives. To get increased enjoyment out of increased resources we need increased character. God has the blueprint for what brings about the most impact and joy. He teaches us this concept with the agricultural imagery of sowing and reaping.

Let's say someone wanted to plant an orange tree in their backyard.

Theoretically, all they would have to do is buy one orange. Then they would plant one seed. The agricultural term for that is "sowing." They would be sowing that seed into the ground with the expectation of "reaping" an orange tree. Eventually when the orange tree matures the person does not simply reap one seed back. They reap an entire crop of oranges each with several seeds inside. Those seeds could again be sown into the ground in order to reap more.

Conceivably, this is how one orange seed could turn into hundreds of orange trees, producing thousands of oranges and hundreds of thousands of orange seeds. Sowing and reaping has a general formula. We sow a little, wait for a time and then reap exponentially more. Imagine if that could be a guarantee with our finances? Astoundingly, God tells us our financial generosity is like that.

The principle of sowing and reaping is tantalizing. Look and see for yourself what God says! Here is what Paul told the Corinthian Christians,

"He who supplies seed to the sower and bread for food will supply and multiply your seed for sowing and increase the harvest of your righteousness. You will be enriched in every way to be generous in every way, which through us will produce thanksgiving to God." (2 Cor 9:10-11)

CHAPTER 4

That is the word of God. When we give we are sowing back to God. In His timing, we will reap much more back.

Why does He give us more back? It is not so that we can vainly pursue the synthetic joy of obtaining more glittery things. We reap more, so we can sow more. This is not a get-rich scheme. It is a way to maximize the purpose and impact of our lives. When someone gives in faith to God, God loves to financially partner with them to build His kingdom. He gives more back not so we can hoard more. He gives more so we can sow more.

This is the difference between what the Bible teaches and what many call "The Prosperity Gospel" or "The Health and Wealth Gospel." The Health and Wealth Gospel teaches that God's desire for each of us is to gain financial riches. The way to get those things is to do the right things and give enough money. The problem is that philosophy uses God like a formula to keep serving the idol of money. When God is on the throne of my life, then I do not give to get more of the world. I give to Him and for His kingdom, out of joy. I sow, to reap more, so I can sow more.

Many believers will tell the same story. They will say it is one of the greatest blessings of giving back to God. They go on the incredible adventure of watching God give back more, so they can give more. If this seems hard to believe, remember Who we are putting our faith in. The same One who is telling us about sowing and reaping financially, is the same One overseeing this agriculturally. He has been successfully accomplishing this on our planet for millennia. Every piece of fruit you have ever eaten, was a product of sowing and reaping. And the development of that piece of fruit was facilitated by the mighty hand of God. He has proven He is more than capable of overseeing this process throughout His creation. Our personal lives are no challenge for Him. The only question then is this: do we have the faith to believe this promise?

BEING RESPONSIBLE

Isn't there a point where giving away money is irresponsible? Doesn't God want us to work hard, plan well and support our families? What if someone is in financial difficulty? This is such an important line of questioning.

There is no doubt that there are so many aspects of how we handle our finances that are important to God. He wants us to be diligent (Prv 10:4). He wants us to plan ahead (Prv 6:6-8). He wants us to overthrow the slavery of debt (Prv 22:7). We should provide for our families (Prv 31:13-18). The Bible celebrates leaving an inheritance to our children (Prv 13:22). So then how do we balance giving back to the Lord with financial responsibility?

Sometimes in the Bible the issue is not one of balance. We can use "balance" as a way of avoiding any kind of extreme. We can pursue balance as a way of making sure things always add up in our minds. But when it comes to God, the issue is not one of balance. It is one of obedience. All of God's ways are fully true, all the time. We just need to submit to how He directs. That will require faith.

Remember God's promises? We test God. In Malachi 3, we are told to bring in the tithe and He pours forth blessing. In Haggai 1, we are called to prioritize the things of God and He responds as the provider. In Matthew 6, Jesus tells us to seek first the kingdom of God and all these things will be added to us. If God rules the universe, then following His commands is always responsible. If there is a Creator that speaks and galaxies burst into existence, then the promise He has spoken about my finances are as sure as the ground beneath my feet, literally. The only irresponsible thing would be neglecting to obey One of such sovereign power.

So no matter what your finances look like right now, step into obedience. No matter what goals you have for saving or getting out of debt, there is One who can easily supply everything you need.

CHAPTER 4

> # He can do more than you can imagine.

So before anything else, prioritize Him. Start with giving a full tithe back to God. Don't wait. Don't miss out on what He can do with your present situation. Don't first strive to get your present situation under control. Let the One who controls the universe, take control of your current situation. And watch what the Sustainer of all things can do.

I want to close with one final story. Any time I get time with my friend Al it is an experience. He's an executive at a well-known South Florida company. But even with his success he's unaffected by it. He's down to earth, casual, funny and even a bit eccentric. He's also a straight shooter. You don't have to wonder what he's thinking. And Al's journey with giving is powerful.

He said it started over 40 years ago. He was in his mid 30s and a new Christian wanting to grow in his faith. He came across this Bible verse in Malachi 3:10, "Bring the full tithe into the storehouse, that there may be food in my house. And thereby put me to the test, says the Lord of hosts, if I will not open the windows of heaven for you and pour down for you a blessing until there is no more need." The directness of the passage struck him. It wasn't complicated. God wanted him to give 10% of his income back to God.

Now, at the time he was making about $400 a week. He did the math. If he tithed he would not be able to pay his electric bill. But if you know Al, he's a pragmatic guy. So to put it in his own words, he said, "I guess I'll just ride this wave of faith and see what God does."

In a step of total faith, he gave $40 that week. And then again after the next paycheck. Why would he do that? If the Bible said it, it had to be true. If he said he believed in the Bible, he better just simply do what it says. By the third week, he received some encouraging news. He was getting a raise… a big raise… a 50% raise. And Al has never looked back. He kept tithing and God kept providing. But that's not the end of his story.

A few years into tithing, a new conviction began to grow. The rest of Malachi 3:10 was enticing him. God tells us to test Him. He says He will "pour down for you a blessing" from heaven, when we give. Can you really out-give God? So, Al put it like this, "I realized that 10% was a minimum. And I'm not a minimum kind of guy. If God blessed me when I gave 10%, what would happen if I gave 11%?" So Al kept going. Here's how he described what kept happening, "Remarkably, or unremarkably, I kept giving and it's mind-boggling how financial blessing shows up in my life." More than 40 years later Al shared that he now far more than a tithe of his income back to God. And to this day, he marvels how God's word has proven true in his life.

CONCLUSION

If we are people of faith, and we say we believe in the Bible, then maybe it's not that complicated. If God spoke and the universe burst into existence, why would we ever question what God said. If this is what God is saying about our finances, how could we not have the faith to take Him at His word? And most importantly, how could we ever hold anything back from my God. He is the Lord. We worship no other God but Him alone. So what could hold us back?

Money naturally tends to be an idol in our lives. Jesus told us it is a showdown that each of us must have. Do we trust in money for security? Do we look to it for happiness? Money as a god will leave us anxious, insecure, discontent, and envious: any idol destroys. Because of the prevalence of money as an idol, God lovingly gives us an ancient practice. He calls us to give to Him first. It gives us a concrete action of faith. And because it is so easy to rationalize, He gives us a crisp clear starting place. He tells us to start with 10%, a tithe. For many this initially seems impossible, but this practice is a fundamental aspect of worship. On top of that, God saturates this faith step with promises. We must simply recalibrate our lives to God's plan and release these tremendous promises in our lives.

Made in the USA
Middletown, DE
19 September 2024